TOPICAL
CONCORDANCE
of Vital

Edited by

D. M. MILLER

LUTTERWORTH PRESS
GUILDFORD, SURREY

ALL RIGHTS RESERVED
These Selections First Published in this Edition 1955
This impression 1984
0 7188 0933 5

CONTENTS

THE TRINITY

TRINITY, THE

Doctrine of, proved from Scripture. *Matt.* 3 : 16, 17. *Rom.* 8 : 9. 1 *Cor.* 12 : 3-6. *Eph.* 4 : 4-6. 1 *Pet.* 1 : 2. 1 *John* 5 : 7. *Jude* 20, 21.

Divine titles applied to the three Persons in. *Exod.* 20 : 2, with *John* 20 : 28, and *Acts* 5 : 3, 4.

Each person in, described as

Eternal. *Rom.* 16 : 26, with *Rev.* 22 : 13. and *Heb.* 9 : 14.

Holy. *Rev.* 4 : 8. *Rev.* 15 : 4, with *Acts* 3 : 14, and 1 *John* 2 : 20.

True. *John* 7 : 28, with *Rev.* 3 : 7, and 1 *John* 5 : 6.

Omnipresent. *Jer.* 23 : 24, with *Eph.* 1 : 23, and *Ps.* 139 : 7.

Omnipotent. *Gen.* 17 : 1, with *Rev.* 1 : 8, and *Rom.* 15 : 19. *Jer.* 32 : 17, with *Heb.* 1 : 3, and *Luke* 1 : 35.

Omniscient. *Acts* 15 : 18, with *John* 22 , 17, and 1 *Cor.* 2 : 10, 11.

Creator. *Gen.* 1 : 1, with *Col.* 1 : 16, and *Job* 33 : 4. *Ps.* 148 : 5, with *John* 1 : 3, and *Job* 26 : 13.

Sanctifier. *Jude* 1, with *Heb.* 2 : 11, and 1 *Pet.* 1 : 2.

Author of all spiritual operations. *Heb.* 13 : 21, with *Col.* 1 : 29, and 1 *Cor.* 12 : 11.

Source of eternal life. *Rom.* 6 : 23, with *John* 10 : 28, and *Gal.* 6 : 8.

Teacher. *Isa.* 54 : 13, with *Luke* 21 : 15, and *John* 14 : 26. *Isa.* 48 : 17, with *Gal.* 1 : 12, and 1 *John* 2 : 20.

Raising Christ from the dead. 1 *Cor.* 6 : 14, with *John* 2 : 19, and 1 *Pet.* 3 : 18.

Inspiring the prophets, etc. *Heb.* 1 : 1, with 2 *Cor.* 13 : 3, and *Mark* 13 : 11.

Supplying ministers to the Church. *Jer.* 3 : 15, with *Eph.* 4 : 11, and *Acts* 20 : 28. *Jer.* 26 : 5, with *Matt.* 10 : 5, and *Acts* 13 : 2.

Salvation the work of. 2 *Thess.* 2 : 13, 14. *Titus* 3 : 4-6. 1 *Pet.* 1 : 2.

Baptism administered in name of. *Matt.* 28 : 19.

Benediction given in name of. 2 *Cor.* 13 ; 14.

Saints

Are the temple of. 2 *Cor.* 6 : 16, with *Eph.* 3 : 17, and 1 *Cor.* 3 : 16. *Eph.* 2 : 22, with *Col.* 1 : 27, and 1 *Cor.* 6 : 19.
Have fellowship with. 1 *John* 1 : 3, with *Phil.* 2 : 1.

Sin, a tempting of. *Deut.* 6 : 16, with 1 *Cor.* 10 : 9, and *Acts* 5 : 9.

The Israelites in the wilderness tempted. *Exod.* 17 : 7, with 1 *Cor.* 10 : 9, and *Heb.* 3 : 7, 9.

GOD THE SON

CHRIST IS GOD

As Jehovah. *Isa.* 40 : 3, with *Matt.* 3 : 3.
As Jehovah of glory. *Ps.* 24 : 7, 10, with 1 *Cor.* 2 : 8. *Jas.* 2 : 1.
As Jehovah, our RIGHTEOUSNESS. *Jer.* 23 : 5, 6, with 1 *Cor.* 1 : 30.
As Jehovah, above all. *Ps.* 97 : 9, with *John* 3 : 31.
As Jehovah, the First and the Last. *Isa.* 44 : 6, with Rev. 1 : 17. *Isa.* 48 : 12-16, with *Rev.* 22 : 13.
As Jehovah's Fellow and Equal. *Zech.* 13 : 7. *Phil.* 2 : 6.
As Jehovah of hosts. *Isa.* 6 : 1-3, with *John* 12 : 41. *Isa.* 8 : 13, 14 with 1 *Pet.* 2 : 8.
As Jehovah of David. *Ps.* 110 : 1, with *Matt.* 22 : 42-45.
As Jehovah, the Shepherd. *Isa.* 40 : 10, 11. *Heb.* 13 : 20.
As Jehovah, for whose glory all things were created. *Prov.* 16 : 4, with *Col.* 1 : 16.
As Jehovah, the Messenger of the covenant. *Mal.* 3 : 1, with *Luke* 2 : 27.
Invoked as Jehovah. *Joel* 2 : 32, with 1 *Cor.* 1 : 2.
As the Eternal God and Creator. *Ps.* 102 : 24-27, with *Heb.* 1 : 8, 10-12.
As the Mighty God. *Isa.* 9 : 6.
As the Great God and Saviour. *Hos.* 1 : 7, with *Titus* 2 : 13.
As God over all. *Rom.* 9 : 5.
As the true God. *Jer.* 10 : 10, with 1 *John* 5 : 20.
As God the Word. *John* 1 : 1.
As God, the Judge. *Eccles.* 12 : 14, with 1 *Cor.* 4 : 5. 2 *Cor.* 5 : 10. 2 *Tim.* 4 : 1.
As Emmanuel. *Isa.* 7 : 14, with *Matt.* 1 : 23.
As King of kings and Lord of lords. *Dan.* 10 : 17, with *Rev.* 1 : 5. *Rev.* 17 : 14.
As the Holy One. 1 *Sam.* 2 : 2, with *Acts* 3 : 14.
As the Lord from heaven. 1 *Cor.* 15 : 47.
As Lord of the sabbath. *Gen.* 2 : 3, with *Matt.* 12 : 8.

As Lord of all. *Acts* 10 : 36. *Rom.* 10 : 11-13.

As Son of God. *Matt.* 26 : 63-67.

As the Only-begotten Son of the Father. *John* 1 : 14, 18. *John* 3 : 16, 18. 1 *John* 4 : 9.

His blood is called the blood of God. *Acts* 20 : 28.

As One with the Father. *John* 10 : 30, 38. *John* 12 : 45. *John* 14 : 7-10. *John* 17 : 10.

As sending the Spirit, equally with the Father. *John* 14 : 16, with *John* 15 : 26.

As entitled to equal honour with the Father. *John* 5 : 23.

As Owner of all things, equally with the Father. *John* 16 : 15.

As unrestricted by the law of the sabbath, equally with the Father. *John* 5 : 17.

As the Source of grace, equally with the Father. 1 *Thess.* 3 : 11. 2 *Thess.* 2 : 16, 17.

As unsearchable, equally with the Father. *Prov.* 30 : 4. *Matt.* 11 : 27.

As Creator of all things. *Isa.* 40 : 28. *John* 1 : 3. *Col.* 1 : 16.

As Supporter and Preserver of all things. *Neh.* 9 : 6, with *Col.* 1 : 17. *Heb.* 1 : 3.

As possessed of the fulness of the Godhead. *Col.* 2 : 9.

As raising the dead. *John* 5 : 21. *John* 6 : 40, 54.

As raising himself from the dead. *John* 2 19, 21. *John* 10 : 18.

As Eternal. *Isa.* 9 : 6. *Mic.* 5 : 2. *John* 1 : 1. *Col.* 1 : 17. *Heb.* 1 : 8-10. *Rev.* 1 : 8.

As Omnipresent. *Matt.* 18 : 20. *Matt.* 28 : 20. *John* 3 : 13.

As Omnipotent. *Ps.* 45 : 3. *Phil.* 3 : 21. *Rev.* 1 : 8.

As Omniscient. *John* 16 : 30. *John* 21 : 17.

As discerning the thoughts of the heart. 1 *Kings* 8 : 39, with *Luke* 5 : 22. *Ezek.* 11 : 5, with *John* 2 : 24, 25. *Rev.* 2 : 23.

As unchangeable. *Mal.* 3 : 6, with *Heb.* 1 : 12. *Heb.* 13 : 8.

As having power to forgive sins. *Col.* 3 : 13, with *Mark* 2 : 7, 10.

As Giver of pastors to the Church. *Jer.* 3 : 15, with *Eph.* 4 : 11-13.

As Husband of the Church. *Isa.* 54 : 5, with *Eph.* 5 : 25-32. *Isa.* 62 : 5, with *Rev.* 21 : 2, 9.

As the object of divine worship. *Acts* 7 : 59. 2 *Cor.* 12 : 8, 9. *Heb.* 1 : 6. *Rev.* 5 : 12.

As the object of faith. *Ps.* 2 : 12, with 1 *Pet.* 2 : 6. *Jer.* 17 : 5, 7, with *John* 14 : 1.

As God, He redeems and purifies the Church unto himself. *Rev.* 5 : 9, with *Titus* 2 : 14.

As God, He presents the Church to himself. *Eph.* 5 : 27, with *Jude* 24 : 25.

Saints live unto him, as God. *Rom.* 6 : 11, and *Gal.* 2 : 19, with 2 *Cor.* 5 : 15.

Acknowledged by his Apostles. *John* 20 : 28.

Acknowledged by Old Testament saints. *Gen.* 17 : 1, with *Gen.* 48 : 15, 16. *Gen.* 32 : 24-30, with *Hos.* 12 : 3-5. *Judges* 6 : 22-24. *Job* 19 : 25-27.

HUMAN NATURE OF CHRIST, THE

Was necessary to his mediatorial office. *1 Tim.* 2 : 5. *Heb.* 2 : 17.

Is proved by his

Conception in the Virgin's womb. *Matt.* 1 : 18. *Luke* 1 : 31.

Birth. *Matt.* 1 : 16, 25. *Matt* 2 : 2. *Luke* 2 : 7, 11.

Partaking of flesh and blood. *John* 1 : 14. *Heb.* 2 : 14.

Having a human soul. *Matt.* 26 : 38. *Luke* 23 : 46. *Acts* 2 : 31.

Circumcision. *Luke* 2 : 21.

Increase in wisdom and stature. *Luke* 2 : 52.

Weeping. *Luke* 19 : 41. *John* 11 : 35.

Hungering. *Matt.* 4 : 2. *Matt.* 21 : 18.

Thirsting. *John* 4 : 7. *John* 19 : 28.

Sleeping. *Matt.* 8 : 24. *Mark* 4 : 38.

Being subject to weariness. *John* 4 : 6.

Being a man of sorrows. *Isa.* 53 : 3, 4. *Luke* 22 : 44. *John* 11 : 33. *John* 12 : 27.

Being buffeted. *Matt.* 26 : 67. *Luke* 22 : 64.

Enduring indignities. *Luke* 23 : 11.

Being scourged. *Matt.* 27 : 26. *John* 19 : 1.

Being nailed to the cross. *Ps.* 22 : 16, with *Luke* 23 : 33.

Death. *John* 19 : 30.

Side being pierced. *John* 19 : 34.

Burial. *Matt.* 27 : 59, 60. *Mark* 15 : 46.

Resurrection. *Acts* 3 : 15. 2 *Tim.* 2 : 8.

Was like our own in all things except sin. *Acts* 3 : 22. *Phil.* 2 : 7, 8. *Heb.* 2 : 17.

Was without sin. *Heb.* 7 : 26, 28. 1 *John* 3 : 5.

Was submitted to the evidence of the senses. *Luke* 24 : 39. *John* 20 : 27. 1 *John* 1 : 1, 2.

Was of the seed of

The woman. *Gen.* 3 : 15. *Isa.* 7 : 14. *Jer.* 31 : 22. *Luke* 1 : 31. *Gal.* 4 : 4.

Abraham. *Gen.* 22 : 18, with *Gal.* 3 : 16. *Heb.* 2 : 16.

David. 2 *Sam.* 7 : 12, 16. *Ps.* 89 : 35, 36. *Jer.* 23 : 5. *Matt.* 22 : 42. *Mark* 10 : 47. *Acts* 2 : 30. *Acts* 13 : 23. *Rom.* 1 : 3.

Genealogy of. *Matt.* 1 : 1, etc. *Luke* 3 : 23, etc.

Attested by himself. *Matt.* 8 : 20. *Matt.* 16 : 13.

Confession of, a test of belonging to God. *John* 4 : 2.

Acknowledged by men. *Mark* 6 : 3. *John* 7 : 27. *John* 19 : 5. *Acts* 2 : 22.

Denied by Antichrist. 1 *John* 4 : 3. 2 *John* 7.

DEATH OF CHRIST, THE

Foretold. *Isa.* 53 : 8. *Dan.* 9 : 26. *Zech.*
13 : 7. *Ps.* 22.
Appointed by God. *Isa.* 53 : 6, 10. *Acts*
2 : 23.
Necessary for the redemption of man. *Luke*
24 : 46. *John* 12 : 24. *Acts* 17 : 3.
Acceptable as a sacrifice to God. *Matt.*
20 : 28. *Eph.* 5 : 2. 1 *Thess.* 5 : 10.
Was voluntary. *Isa.* 53 : 12. *Matt.* 26 :
53. *John* 10 : 17, 18.
Was undeserved. *Isa.* 53 : 9.

Mode of

Foretold by Christ. *Matt.* 20 : 18, 19.
John 12 : 32, 33.
Prefigured. *Num.* 21 : 8, with *John* 3 :
14.
Ignominious. *Heb.* 12 : 2.
Accursed. *Deut.* 21 : 23. *Gal.* 3 : 13.
Exhibited his humility. *Phil.* 2 : 8.
A stumbling-block to Jews. 1 *Cor.* 1
23.
Foolishness to Gentiles. 1 *Cor.* 1 : 18,
23.

Demanded by the Jews. *Matt.* 27 : 22, 23.
Inflicted by the Gentiles. *Matt.* 27 : 26-35.
In the company of malefactors. *Isa.*
53 : 12, with *Matt.* 27 : 38.
Accompanied by preternatural signs. *Matt.*
27 : 45, 51-53.
Emblematical of the death unto sin. *Rom.*
6 : 3-8. *Gal.* 2 : 20.
Commemorated in the sacrament of the
Lord's Supper. *Luke* 22 : 19, 20.

RESURRECTION OF CHRIST,
THE

Foretold by the prophets. *Ps.* 16 : 10,
with *Acts* 13 : 34, 35. *Isa.* 26 : 19.
Foretold by himself. *Matt.* 20 : 19. *Mark*
9 : 9. *Mark* 14 : 28. *John* 2 : 19-22.

Was necessary to

The fulfilment of scripture. *Luke* 24 :
45, 46.
Forgiveness of sins. 1 *Cor.* 15 : 17.
Justification. *Rom.* 4 : 25. *Rom.* 8 : 34.
Hope. 1 *Cor.* 15 : 19.
The efficacy of preaching. 1 *Cor.* 15 : 14.
The efficacy of faith. 1 *Cor.* 15 : 14, 17.
A proof of his being the Son of God. *Ps.*
2 : 7, with *Acts* 13 : 33. *Rom.* 1 : 4.

Effected by

The power of God. *Acts* 2 : 24. *Acts*
3 : 15. *Rom.* 8 : 11. *Eph.* 1 : 20. *Col.*
2 : 12.
His own power. *John* 2 : 19. *John* 10 : 18.
The power of the Holy Ghost. 1 *Pet.*
3 : 18.
On the first day of the week. *Mark* 16 :
9.

On the third day after his death. *Luke*
24 : 46. *Acts* 10 : 40. 1 *Cor.* 15 : 4. *Gen.*
1 : 11-13. *Gen.* 22 : 4, 5. *Gen.* 40 : 20.
Gen. 42 : 18. *Exod.* 3 : 18. *Exod.* 15 : 1.
Lev. 23 : 11. *Num.* 19 : 12. *Esther* 4 : 16.
Esther 5 : 1, 2.

The Apostles

At first did not understand the pre-
dictions respecting. *Mark* 9 : 10.
John 20 : 9.
Very slow to believe. *Mark* 16 : 13.
Luke 24 : 9, 11, 37, 38.
Reproved for their unbelief of. *Mark*
16 : 14.

He appeared after, to

Mary Magdalene. *Mark* 16 : 9. *John*
20 : 18.
The women. *Matt.* 28 : 9.
Simon Peter. *Luke* 24 : 34.
Two disciples. *Luke* 24 : 13-31.
Apostles, except Thomas. *John* 20 : 19,
24.
Apostles, Thomas being present. *John*
20 : 26.
Apostles at the sea of Tiberias. *John*
21 : 1.
Apostles in Galilee. *Matt.* 28 : 16, 17.
Above five hundred brethren. 1 *Cor.*
15 : 6.
James. 1 *Cor.* 15 : 7.
All the Apostles. *Luke* 24 : 51. *Acts*
1 : 9. 1 *Cor.* 15 : 7.
Paul. 1 *Cor.* 15 : 8.
Fraud impossible in. *Matt.* 27 : 63-66.
He gave many infallible proofs of. *Luke*
24 : 35, 39, 43. *John* 20 : 20, 27. *Acts* 1 :
3.

Was attested by

Angels. *Matt.* 28 : 5-7. *Luke* 24 : 4-7,
23.
Apostles. *Acts* 1 : 22. *Acts* 2 : 32. *Acts*
3 : 15. *Acts* 4 : 33.
His enemies. *Matt.* 28 : 11-15.
Asserted and preached by the Apostles.
Acts 25 : 19. *Acts* 26 : 23.

Saints

Begotten to a lively hope by. 1 *Pet.* 1 :
3, 21.
Desire to know the power of. *Phil.* 3 :
10.
Should keep, in remembrance. 2 *Tim.*
2 : 8.
Shall rise in the likeness of. *Rom.* 6 : 5.
1 *Cor.* 15 : 49, with *Phil.* 3 : 21.
Is an emblem of the new birth. *Rom.* 6 : 4.
Col. 2 : 12.
The first-fruits of our resurrection. *Acts*
26 : 23. 1 *Cor.* 15 : 20, 23.
The truth of the gospel involved in. 1 *Cor.*
15 : 14, 15.
Followed by his exaltation. *Acts* 4 : 10, 11.
Rom. 8 : 34. *Eph.* 1 : 20. *Rev.* 1 : 18.

An assurance of the judgment. *Acts* 1: 31.

Typified. ISAAC, *Gen.* 22 : 13, with *Heb.* 11: 19. JONAH, *Jonah* 2 : 10. with *Matt.* 12 : 40.

GOD THE HOLY SPIRIT

HOLY SPIRIT, THE, IS GOD

As Jehovah. *Exod.* 17 : 7, with *Heb.* 3 : 7-9. *Num.* 12 : 6, with 2 *Pet.* 1 : 21.

As Jehovah of hosts. *Isa.* 6 : 3, 8-10, with *Acts* 28 : 25.

As Jehovah, Most High. *Ps.* 78 : 17, 21, with *Acts* 7 : 51.

Being invoked as Jehovah. *Luke* 2 : 26-29. *Acts* 4 : 23-25, with *Acts* 1 : 16, 20. 2 *Thess.* 3 : 5.

As called God. *Acts* 5 : 3, 4.

As eternal. *Heb.* 9 : 14.

As omnipresent. *Ps.* 139 : 7-13.

As omniscient. 1 *Cor.* 2 : 10.

As omnipotent. *Luke* 1 : 35. *Rom.* 15 : 19.

As the Spirit of glory and of God. 1 *Pet.* 4 : 14.

As Creator. *Gen.* 1 : 26, 27, with *Job* 33 : 4.

As equal to, and one with the Father. *Matt.* 28 : 19. 2 *Cor.* 13 : 14.

As Sovereign Disposer of all things. *Dan.* 4 : 35, with *Cor.* 12 : 6, 11.

As Author of the new birth. *John* 3 : 5, 6, with 1 *John* 5 : 4.

As raising Christ from the dead. *Acts* 2 : 24, with 1 *Pet.* 3 : 18. *Heb.* 13 : 20, with *Rom.* 1: 4.

As inspiring scripture. 2 *Tim.* 3 : 16, with 2 *Pet.* 1 : 21.

As the source of wisdom. 1 *Cor.* 12 : 8.

As the source of miraculous power. *Matt.* 12 : 28, with *Luke* 11 : 20. *Acts* 19 : 11, with *Rom.* 15 : 19.

As appointing and sending ministers. *Acts* 13 : 2, 4, with *Matt.* 9 : 38. *Acts* 20 : 28.

As directing where the gospel should be preached. *Acts* 16 : 6, 7, 10.

As dwelling in saints. *John* 14 : 17, with 1 *Cor.* 14 : 25. 1 *Cor.* 3 : 16, with 1 *Cor.* 6 : 19.

As Comforter of the Church. *Acts* 9 : 31, with 2 *Cor.* 1 : 3.

As sanctifying the Church. *Ezek.* 37 : 28, with *Rom.* 15 : 16.

As the Witness. *Heb.* 10 : 15, with 1 *John* 5 : 9.

HOLY SPIRIT, THE COMFORTER, THE

Proceeds from the Father. *John* 15 : 26.

Given

    By the Father. *John* 14 : 16.

    By Christ. *Isa.* 61 : 3.

    Through Christ's intercession. *John* 14:16.

9

Sent in the name of Christ. *John* 14 : 26.
Sent by Christ from the Father. *John* 15 :
26. *John* 16 : 7.

As such he
Communicates joy to saints. *Rom.* 14 :
17. *Gal.* 5 : 22. 1 *Thess.* 1 : 6.
Edifies the Church. *Acts* 9 : 31.
Testifies of Christ. *John* 15 : 26.
Imparts the love of God. *Rom.* 5 : 3-5.
Imparts hope. *Rom.* 15 : 13. *Gal* 5 : 5.
Teaches saints. *John* 14 : 26.
Dwells with, and in saints. *John* 14 : 17.
Abides for ever with saints. *John* 14 : 16.
Is known by saints. *John* 14 : 17.
The world cannot receive. *John* 14 : 17.

HOLY SPIRIT, THE TEACHER, THE

Promised. *Prov.* 1 : 23.
As the Spirit of wisdom. *Isa.* 11 : 2. *Isa.*
40 : 13, 14.

Given
In answer to prayer. *Eph.* 1 : 16, 17.
To saints. *Neh.* 9 : 20. 1 *Cor.* 2 : 12, 13.
Necessity for. 1 *Cor.* 2 : 9, 10.

As such he
Reveals the things of God. 1 *Cor.* 10 : 13.
Reveals the things of Christ. *John* 16 :
14.
Brings the words of Christ to remem-
brance. *John* 14 : 26.
Directs in the way of godliness. *Isa.* 30 :
21. *Ezek.* 36 : 27.
Teaches saints to answer persecutors.
Mark 13 : 11. *Luke* 12 : 12.
Enables ministers to teach. 1 *Cor.* 12 : 8.
Guides into all truth. *John* 14 : 26.
John 16 : 13.
Attend to the instruction of. *Rev.* 2 : 7,
11, 29.
The natural man will not receive the things
of. 1 *Cor.* 2 : 14.

THE SCRIPTURES

SCRIPTURES, THE

Given by inspiration of God. 2 *Tim.* 3 : 16.
Given by inspiration of the Holy Ghost.
Acts 1 : 16, *Heb.* 3 : 7. 2 *Pet.* 1 : 21.
Christ sanctioned, by appealing to them.
Matt. 4 : 4. *Mark* 12 : 10. *John* 7 : 42.
Christ taught out of. *Luke* 24 : 27.

Are called the
Word. *Jas.* 1 : 21-23. 1 *Pet.* 2 : 2.
Word of God. *Luke* 11 : 28. *Heb.* 4 : 12.
Word of Christ. *Col.* 3 : 16.
Word of truth. *Jas.* 1 : 18.
Holy scriptures. *Rom.* 1 : 2. 2 *Tim.*
3 : 15.

Scripture of truth. *Dan.* 10 : 21.
Book. *Ps.* 40 : 7. *Rev.* 22 : 19.
Book of the Lord. *Isa.* 34 : 16.
Book of the law. *Neh.* 8 : 3. *Gal.* 3 : 10.
Law of the Lord. *Ps.* 1 : 2. *Isa.* 30 : 9.
Sword of the Spirit. *Eph.* 6 : 17.
Oracles of God. *Rom.* 3 : 2. 1 *Pet.* 4 : 11.
Contain the promises of the gospel. *Rom.* 1 : 2.
Reveal the laws, statutes, and judgments of God. *Deut.* 4 : 5, 14, with *Exod.* 24 : 3, 4.
Record divine prophecies. *Is.* 1 : 19-21.
Testify of Christ. *John* 5 : 39. *Acts* 10 : 43. *Acts* 18 : 28. 1 *Cor.* 15 : 3.
Are full and sufficient. *Luke* 16 : 29, 31.
Are an unerring guide. *Prov.* 6 : 23. 2 *Pet.* 1 : 19.
Are able to make wise unto salvation through faith in Christ Jesus. 2 *Tim.* 3 : 15.
Are profitable both for doctrine and practice. 2 *Tim.* 3 : 16, 17.

Described as

Pure. *Ps.* 12 : 6. *Ps.* 119 : 140. *Prov.* 30 : 5.
True. *Ps.* 119 : 169. *John* 17 : 17.
Perfect. *Ps.* 19 : 7.
Precious. *Ps.* 19 : 10.
Quick and powerful. *Heb.* 4 : 12.
Written for our instruction. *Rom.* 15 : 4.
Intended for the use of all men. *Rom.* 16 : 26.
Nothing to be taken from, or added to *Deut.* 4 : 2. *Deut.* 12 : 32. *Prov.* 30 : 5, 6. *Rev.* 22 : 18, 19.
One portion of, to be compared with another. 1 *Cor.* 2 : 13.

Designed for

Regenerating. *Jas.* 1 : 18. 1 *Pet.* 1 : 23.
Quickening. *Ps.* 119 : 50, 93.
Illuminating. *Ps.* 119 : 130.
Converting the soul. *Ps.* 19 : 7.
Making wise the simple. *Ps.* 19 : 7.
Sanctifying. *John* 17 : 17. *Eph.* 5 : 26.
Producing faith. *John* 20 : 31.
Producing hope. *Ps.* 119 : 49. *Rom.* 15 : 4.
Producing obedience. *Deut.* 17 : 19, 20.
Cleansing the heart. *John* 15 : 3. *Eph.* 5 : 26.
Cleansing the ways. *Ps.* 119 : 9.
Keeping from destructive paths. *Ps.* 17 : 4.
Supporting life. *Deut.* 8 : 3, with *Matt.* 4 : 4.
Promoting growth in grace. 1 *Pet.* 2 : 2.
Building up in the faith. *Acts* 20 : 32.
Admonishing. *Ps.* 19 : 14. 1 *Cor.* 10 : 11.
Comforting. *Ps.* 119 : 82. *Rom.* 15 : 4.
Rejoicing the heart. *Ps.* 19 : 8. *Ps.* 119 : 111.
Work effectually in them that believe. 1 *Thess.* 2 : 13.

The letter of, without the spirit, killeth. *John* 6 : 63, with 2 *Cor.* 3 : 6.
Ignorance of, a source of error. *Matt.* 22 : 29. *Acts* 13 : 27.
Christ enables us to understand. *Luke* 24 : 45.
The Holy Ghost enables us to understand. *John.* 16 : 13. 1 *Cor.* 2 : 10-14.
No prophecy of, is of any private interpretation. 2 *Pet.* 1 : 20.
Everything should be tried by. *Isa.* 8 : 20. *Acts* 17 : 11.

Should be

The standard of teaching. 1 *Pet.* 4 : 11.
Believed. *John* 2 : 22.
Appealed to. 1 *Cor.* 1 : 31. 1 *Pet.* 1 : 16.
Read. *Deut.* 17 : 19. *Isa.* 34 : 16.
Read publicly to ALL. *Deut.* 31 : 11-13. *Neh.* 8 : 3. *Jer.* 36 : 6. *Acts* 13 : 15.
Known. 2 *Tim.* 3 : 15.
Received, not as the word of men, but as the word of God. 1 *Thess.* 2 : 13.
Received with meekness. *Jas.* 1 : 21.
Searched. *John* 5 : 39. *John* 7 : 52.
Searched daily. *Acts* 17 : 11.
Laid up in the heart. *Deut.* 6 : 6. *Deut.* 11 : 18.
Taught to children. *Deut.* 6 : 7. *Deut.* 11 : 19. 2 *Tim.* 3 : 15.
Taught to ALL. 2 *Chron.* 17 : 7-9. *Neh.* 8 : 7, 8.
Talked of continually. *Deut.* 6 : 7.
Not handled deceitfully. 2 *Cor.* 4 : 2.
Not only heard, but obeyed. *Matt.* 7 : 24, with *Luke* 11 : 28. *Jas.* 1 : 22.
Used against our spiritual enemies. *Matt.* 4 : 4, 7, 10, with *Eph.* 6 : 11, 17.
All should desire to hear. *Neh.* 8 : 1.
Mere hearers of, deceive themselves. *Jas.* 1 : 22.
Advantage of possessing. *Rom.* 3 : 2.

Saints

Love exceedingly. *Ps.* 119 : 97, 113, 159, 167.
Delight in. *Ps.* 1 : 2.
Regard, as sweet. *Ps.* 119 : 103.
Esteem, above all things. *Job* 23 : 12.
Long after. *Ps.* 119 : 82.
Stand in awe of. *Ps.* 119 : 161. *Isa.* 66 : 2.
Keep, in remembrance. *Ps.* 119 : 16.
Grieve when men disobey. *Ps.* 119 : 158.
Hide, in their heart. *Ps.* 119 : 11.
Hope in. *Ps.* 119 : 74, 81, 147.
Meditate in. *Ps.* 1 : 2. *Ps.* 119 : 99, 148.
Rejoice in. *Ps.* 119 : 162. *Jer.* 15 : 16.
Trust in. *Ps.* 119 : 42.
Obey. *Ps.* 119 : 67. *Luke* 8 : 21. *John* 17 : 6.
Speak of. *Ps.* 119 : 172.
Esteem, as a light. *Ps.* 119 : 105.
Pray to be taught. *Ps.* 119 : 12, 18, 33, 66.
Pray to be conformed to. *Ps.* 119 : 133.

Plead the promises of, in prayer. *Ps.*
119 : 25, 28, 41, 76, 169.
They who search, are truly noble. *Acts*
17 : 11.
Blessedness of hearing and obeying. *Luke*
11 : 28. *Jas.* 1 : 25.
Let them dwell richly in you. *Col.* 3 : 16.

CREATION

CREATION

The formation of things which had no
previous existence. *Rom.* 4 : 17, with
Heb. 11 : 3.

Effected

By God. *Gen.* 1 : 1. *Gen.* 2 : 4, 5. *Prov.*
26 : 10.
By Christ. *John* 1 : 3, 10. *Col.* 1 : 16.
By the Holy Ghost. *Job* 26 : 13. *Ps.*
104 : 30.
By the command of God. *Ps.* 30 : 9.
Heb. 11 : 3.
In the beginning. *Gen.* 1 : 1. *Matt.* 24 :
21.
In six days. *Exod.* 20 : 11. *Exod.* 31 : 17.
According to God's purpose. *Ps.* 135 : 6.
For God's pleasure. *Prov.* 16 : 4. *Rev.*
4 : 11.
For Christ. *Col.* 1 : 16.
By faith we believe, to be God's work
Heb. 11 : 3.

Order of :

First day, making light and dividing it
from darkness. *Gen.* 1 : 3-5. 2 *Cor.*
4 : 6.
Second day, making the firmament or
atmosphere, and separating the waters.
Gen. 1 : 6-8.
Third day, separating the land from
the water, and making it fruitful. *Gen.*
1 : 9-13.
Fourth day, placing the sun, moon, and
stars to give light, &c. *Gen.* 1 : 14-19.
Fifth day, making birds, insects, and
fishes. *Gen.* 1 : 20-23.
Sixth day, making beasts of the earth
and man. *Gen.* 1 : 24, 28.
God rested from, on the seventh day.
Gen. 2 : 2, 3.
Approved of by God. *Gen.* 1 : 31.
A subject of joy to angels. *Job* 38 : 7.

Exhibits

The deity of God. *Rom.* 1 : 20.
The power of God. *Isa.* 40 : 26, 28.
Rom. 1 : 20.
The glory and handywork of God. *Ps.*
19 : 1.
The wisdom of God. *Ps.* 104 : 24. *Ps.*
136 : 5.

13

THE FALL OF MAN

FALL OF MAN, THE

By the disobedience of Adam. *Gen.* 3 : 6, 11, 12, with *Rom.* 5 : 12, 15, 19.
Through temptation of the devil. *Gen.* 3 1-5. 2 *Cor.* 11 : 3. 1 *Tim.* 2 : 14.

Man in consequence of ;
Made in the image of Adam. *Gen.* 5 : 3, with 1 *Cor.* 15 : 48, 49.
Born in sin. *Job* 25 : 4. *Ps.* 51 : 5. *Isa.* 48 : 8. *John* 3 : 6.
A child of the devil. *Matt.* 13 : 38. *John* 8 : 44. 1 *John* 3 : 8, 10.
A child of wrath. *Eph.* 2 : 3.
Evil in heart. *Gen.* 6 : 5. *Gen.* 8 : 21. *Jer.* 16 : 12. *Matt.* 15 : 19.
Blinded in heart. *Eph.* 4 : 18.
Corrupt and perverse in his ways. *Gen.* 6 : 12. *Ps.* 10 : 5. *Rom.* 3 : 12-16.
Depraved in mind. *Rom.* 8 : 5-7. *Eph.* 4 : 17. *Col.* 1 : 21. *Titus* 1 : 15.
Without understanding. *Ps.* 14 : 2, 3, with *Rom.* 3 : 11. *Rom.* 1 : 31.
Receives not the things of God. 1 *Cor.* 2 : 14.
Comes short of God's glory. *Rom.* 3 : 23.
Defiled in conscience. *Titus* 1 : 15. *Heb.* 10 : 22.
Intractable. *Job* 11 : 12.
Estranged from God. *Gen.* 3 : 8. *Ps.* 58 : 3. *Eph.* 4 : 18. *Col.* 1 : 21.
In bondage to sin. *Rom.* 6 : 19. *Rom.* 7 : 5, 23. *Gal.* 5 : 17. *Titus* 3 : 3.
In bondage to the devil. 2 *Tim.* 2 : 26. *Heb.* 2 : 14, 15.
Constant in evil. *Ps.* 10 : 5. 2 *Pet.* 2 : 14.
Conscious of guilt. *Gen.* 3 : 7, 8, 10.
Unrighteous. *Eccles.* 7 : 20. *Rom.* 3 : 10.
Abominable. *Job* 15 : 16. *Ps.* 14 : 3.
Turned to his own way. *Isa.* 53 : 6.
Loves darkness. *John* 3 : 19.
Corrupt, &c. in speech. *Rom.* 3 : 13, 14.
Destructive. *Rom.* 3 : 15, 16.
Devoid of the fear of God. *Rom.* 3 : 18.
Totally depraved. *Gen.* 6 : 5. *Rom.* 7 18.
Dead in sin. *Eph.* 2 : 1. *Col.* 2 : 13.
All men partake of the effects of. 1 *Kings* 8 : 46. *Gal.* 3 : 22. 1 *John* 1 : 8. 1 *John* 5 : 19.

Punishment consequent upon
Banishment from paradise. *Gen.* 3 : 24.
Condemnation to labour and sorrow. *Gen.* 3 : 16, 19. *Job* 5 : 6, 7.
Temporal death. *Gen.* 3 : 19. *Rom.* 5: 12. 1 *Cor.* 15 : 22.
Eternal death. *Job* 21 : 30. *Rom.* 5 : 18, 21. *Rom.* 6 : 23.
Cannot be remedied by man. *Prov.* 20 : 9. *Jer.* 2 : 22. *Jer.* 13 : 23.
Remedy for, provided by God. *Gen.* 3 : 15.

THE ATONEMENT

ATONEMENT, THE

Explained. *Rom.* 5 : 8-11. 2 *Cor.* 5 : 18,19. *Gal.* 1 : 4. 1 *John* 2 : 2. 1 *John* 4 : 10.

Foreordained. *Rom.* 3 : 25. (Margin) 1 *Pet.* 1 : 11, 20. *Rev.* 13 : 8.

Foretold. *Isa.* 53 : 4-6, 8-12. *Dan.* 9 : 24-27. *Zech.* 13 : 1, 7. *John* 11 : 50, 51.

Effected by Christ alone. *John* 1 : 29, 36. *Acts* 4 : 10, 12. 1 *Thess.* 1 : 10. 1 *Tim.* 2 : 5, 6. *Heb.* 2 : 9. 1 *Pet.* 2 : 24.

Was voluntary. *Ps.* 40 : 6-8, with *Heb.* 10 : 5-9. *John* 10 : 11, 15, 17, 18.

Exhibits the

Grace and mercy of God. *Rom.* 8 : 32. *Eph.* 2 : 4, 5, 7. 1 *Tim.* 2 : 4. *Heb.* 2 : 9.

Love of God. *Rom.* 5 : 8. 1 *John* 4 : 9, 10.

Love of Christ. *John* 15 : 13. *Gal.* 2 : 20. *Eph.* 5 : 2, 25. *Rev.* 1 : 5.

Reconciles the justice and mercy of God. *Isa.* 45 : 21. *Rom.* 3 : 25, 26.

Necessity for. *Luke* 19 : 10. *Heb.* 9 : 22.

Made but once. *Heb.* 7 : 27. *Heb.* 9 : 24-28. *Heb.* 10 : 10, 12, 14. 1 *Pet.* 3 : 18.

Acceptable to God. *Eph.* 5 : 2.

Reconciliation to God effected by. *Rom.* 5 : 10. 2 *Cor.* 5 : 18-20. *Eph.* 2 : 13-16. *Col.* 1 : 20-22. *Heb.* 2 : 17. 1 *Pet.* 3 : 18.

Access to God by. *Heb.* 10 : 19, 20.

Remission of sins by. *John* 1 : 29. *Rom.* 3 : 25. *Eph.* 1 : 7. 1 *John* 1 : 7. *Rev.* 1 : 5.

Justification by. *Rom.* 5 : 9. 2 *Cor.* 5 : 21.

Sanctification by. 2 *Cor.* 5 : 15. *Eph.* 5 : 26, 27. *Titus* 2 : 14. *Heb.* 10 : 10. *Heb.* 13 : 12.

Redemption by. *Matt.* 20 : 28. 1 *Tim.* 2 : 6. *Heb.* 9 : 12. *Rev.* 5 : 9.

Has delivered saints from the

Power of sin. *Rom.* 8 : 3. 1 *Pet.* 1 : 18, 19.

Power of the World. *Gal.* 1 : 4. *Gal.* 6 : 14.

Power of the devil. *Col.* 2 : 15. *Heb.* 2 : 14, 15.

Saints glorify God for. 1 *Cor.* 6 : 20. *Gal.* 2 : 20. *Phil.* 1 : 20, 21.

Saints rejoice in God for. *Rom.* 5 : 11.

Saints praise God for. *Rev.* 5 : 9-13.

Faith in, indispensable. *Rom.* 3 : 25. *Gal.* 3 : 13, 14.

Commemorated in the Lord's Supper. *Matt.* 26 : 26-28. 1 *Cor.* 11 : 23-26.

Ministers should fully set forth. *Acts* 5 : 29-31, 42. 1 *Cor.* 15 : 3. 2 *Cor.* 5 : 18-21.

Typified. *Gen.* 4 : 4, with *Heb.* 11 : 4. *Gen.* 22 : 2, with *Heb.* 11 : 17, 19. *Exod.* 12 : 5, 11, 14, with 1 *Cor.* 5 : 7. *Exod.* 24 : 8, with *Heb.* 9 : 20. *Lev.* 16 : 30, 34, with *Heb.* 9 : 7, 12, 28. *Lev.* 17 : 11, with *Heb.* 9 : 22.

REGENERATION

NEW BIRTH, THE

The corruption of human nature requires.
John 3 : 6. *Rom.* 8 : 7, 8.
None can enter heaven without. *John* 3 : 3.

Effected by

God. *John* 1 : 13. 1 *Pet.* 1 : 3.
Christ. 1 *John* 2 : 29.
The Holy Ghost. *John* 3 : 6. *Titus* 3 : 5.

Through the instrumentality of

The word of God. *Jas.* 1 : 18. 1 *Pet.* 1 : 23.
The resurrection of Christ. 1 *Pet.* 1 : 3.
The ministry of the gospel. 1 *Cor.* 4 : 15.
Is of the will of God. *Jas.* 1 : 18.
Is of the mercy of God. *Titus* 3 : 5.
Is for the glory of God. *Isa.* 43 : 7.

Described as

A new creation. 2 *Cor.* 5 : 17. *Gal.* 6 : 15. *Eph.* 2 : 10.
Newness of life. *Rom.* 6 : 4.
A spiritual resurrection. *Rom.* 6 : 4-6. *Eph.* 2 : 1, 5. *Col.* 2 : 12. *Col.* 3 : 1.
A new heart. *Ezek.* 36 : 26.
A new spirit. *Ezek.* 11 : 19. *Rom.* 7 : 6.
Putting on the new man. *Eph.* 4 : 24.
The inward man. *Rom.* 7 : 22. 2 *Cor.* 4 : 16.
Circumcision of the heart. *Deut.* 30 : 6. with *Rom.* 2 : 29. *Col.* 2 : 11.
Partaking of the divine nature. 2 *Pet.* 1 : 4.
The washing of regeneration. *Titus* 3 : 5.
All saints partake of. 1 *Pet.* 2 : 2. 1 *John* 5 : 1.

Produces

Likeness to God. *Eph.* 4 : 24. *Col.* 3 : 10.
Likeness to Christ. *Rom.* 8 : 29.
Knowledge of God. *Jer.* 24 : 7. *Col.* 3 : 10.
Hatred of sin. 1 *John* 3 : 9. 1 *John* 5 : 18.
Victory over the world. 1 *John* 5 : 4.
Delight in God's law. *Rom.* 7 : 22.

Evidenced by

Faith in Christ. 1 *John* 5 : 1.
Righteousness. 1 *John* 2 : 29.
Brotherly love. 1 *John* 4 : 7.
Connected with adoption. *Isa.* 43 : 6, 7. *John* 1 : 12, 13.
The ignorant cavil at. *John* 3 : 4.
Manner of effecting—Illustrated. *John* 3 : 8.
Preserves from satan's devices. 1 *John* 5 : 18.

REDEMPTION

REDEMPTION

Defined. 1 *Cor.* 7 : 23.
Is of God. *Isa.* 44 : 21-23, with *Luke* 1 : 68.
Is by Christ. *Matt.* 20 : 28. *Gal.* 3 : 13.
Is by the blood of Christ. *Acts* 20 : 28.
Heb. 9 : 12. 1 *Pet.* 1 : 19. *Rev.* 5 : 9.
Christ sent to effect. *Gal.* 4 : 4, 5.
Christ is made, unto us. 1 *Cor.* 1 : 30.

Is from

The bondage of the law. *Gal.* 4 : 5.
The curse of the law. *Gal.* 3 : 13.
The power of sin. *Rom.* 6 : 18, 22.
The power of the grave. *Ps.* 49 : 15.
All troubles. *Ps.* 25 : 22.
All iniquity. *Ps.* 130 : 8. *Titus* 2 : 14.
All evil. *Gen.* 48 : 16.
This present evil world. *Gal.* 1 : 4.
Vain conversation. 1 *Pet.* 1 : 18.
Enemies. *Ps.* 106 : 10, 11. *Jer.* 15 : 21.
Death. *Hos.* 13 : 14.
Destruction. *Ps.* 103 : 4.
Man cannot effect. *Ps.* 49 : 7.
Corruptible things cannot purchase. 1
Pet. 1 : 18.

Procures for us

Justification. *Rom.* 3 : 24.
Forgiveness of sin. *Eph.* 1 : 7 *Col.* 1 : 14.
Adoption. *Gal.* 4 : 4, 5.
Purification. *Titus* 2 : 14.
The present life, the only season for. *Job*
36 : 18, 19.

Described as

Precious. *Ps.* 49 : 8.
Plenteous. *Ps.* 130 : 7.
Eternal. *Heb.* 9 : 12.

Subjects of,

The soul. *Ps.* 49 : 15. *Ps.* 71 : 23.
The body. *Rom.* 8 : 23.
The life. *Ps.* 103 : 4. *Lam.* 3 : 58.
The inheritance. *Eph.* 1 : 14.

Manifests the

Power of God. *Isa.* 50 : 2.
Grace of God. *Isa.* 52 : 3.
Love and pity of God. *Isa.* 63 : 9.
A subject for praise. *Isa.* 44 : 22, 23. *Isa.*
51 : 11.
Old Testament saints partakers of. *Heb.*
9 : 15.

They who partake of,

Are the property of God. *Isa.* 43 : 1.
1 *Cor.* 6 : 20.
Are first-fruits unto God. *Rev.* 14 : 4.
Are a peculiar people. 2 *Sam.* 7 : 23.
Titus 2 : 14, with 1 *Pet.* 2 : 9.
Are assured of. *Job* 19 : 25. *Ps.* 31 : 5.
Are sealed unto the day of. *Eph.* 4 : 30.
Are zealous of good works. *Titus* 2 : 14.
Walk safely in holiness. *Isa.* 35 : 8, 9.
Shall return to Zion with joy. *Isa.* 35 :
10.

Alone can learn the songs of heaven.
Rev. 14 : 3, 4.
Commit themselves to God. *Ps.* 31 : 5.
Have an earnest of the completion of.
Eph. 1 : 14, with 2 *Cor.* 1 : 22.
Wait for the completion of. *Rom.* 8 : 23.
Pray for the completion of. *Ps.* 26 : 11.
Ps. 44 : 26.
Praise God for. *Ps.* 71 : 23. *Rev.* 5 : 9.
Should glorify God for. 1 *Cor.* 6 : 20.
Should be without fear. *Isa.* 43 : 1.
Typified. ISRAEL, *Exod.* 6 : 6. FIRST-BORN,
Exod. 13 : 11-15. *Num.* 18 : 15. ATONE-
MENT-MONEY, *Exod.* 30 : 12-15. BOND-
SERVANT, *Lev.* 25 : 47-54.

SANCTIFICATION

Is separation to the service of God. *Ps.*
4 : 3. 2 *Cor.* 6 : 17.

Effected by
  God. *Ezek.* 37 : 28. 1 *Thess.* 5 : 23.
    Jude 1.
  Christ. *Heb.* 2 : 11. *Heb.* 13 : 12.
  The Holy Ghost. *Rom.* 15 : 16. 1 *Cor.*
    6 : 11.
In Christ. 1 *Cor.* 1 : 2.
Through the atonement of Christ. *Heb.*
  10 : 10. *Heb.* 13 : 12.
Through the word of God. *John* 17 : 17,
  19. *Eph.* 5 : 26.
Christ made, of God, unto us. 1 *Cor.* 1 : 30.
Saints elected to salvation through. 2
  Thess. 2 : 13. 1 *Pet.* 1 : 2.
All saints are in a state of. *Acts* 20 : 32.
  Acts 26 : 18. 1 *Cor.* 6 : 11.
The Church made glorious by. *Eph.* 5 : 26,
  27.

Should lead to
  Mortification of sin. 1 *Thess.* 4 : 3, 4.
  Holiness. *Rom.* 6 : 22. *Eph.* 5 : 7-9.
Offering up of saints acceptable through.
  Rom. 15 : 16.
Saints fitted for the service of God by.
  2 *Tim.* 2 : 21.
God wills all saints to have. 1 *Thess.* 4 : 3.

ASSURANCE OF SALVATION

ASSURANCE

Produced by faith. *Eph.* 3 : 12. 2 *Tim.*
  1 : 12. *Heb.* 10 : 22.
Made full by hope. *Heb.* 6 : 11, 19.
Confirmed by love. 1 *John* 3 : 14, 19. 1
  John 4 : 18.
Is the effect of righteousness. *Isa.* 32 : 17.
Is abundant in the understanding of the
  gospel. *Col.* 2 : 2. 1 *Thess.* 1 : 5.

Saints privileged to have, of

Their election. *Ps.* 4 : 3. 1 *Thess.* 1 : 4.
Their redemption. *Job* 19 : 25.
Their adoption. *Rom.* 8 : 16. 1 *John* 3 : 2.
Their salvation. *Isa.* 12 : 2.
Eternal life. 1 *John* 5 : 13.
The unalienable love of God. *Rom.* 8 : 38, 39.
Union with God and Christ. 1 *Cor.* 6 : 15. 2 *Cor.* 13 : 5. *Eph.* 5 : 30. 1 *John* 2 : 5. 1 *John* 4 : 13.
Peace with God by Christ. *Rom.* 5 : 1.
Preservation. *Ps.* 3 : 6, 8. *Ps.* 27 : 3-5. *Ps.* 46 : 1-3.
Answers to prayer. 1 *John* 3 : 22. 1 *John* 5 : 14, 15.
Continuance in grace. *Phil.* 1 : 6.
Comfort in affliction. *Ps.* 73 : 26. *Luke* 4 : 18, 19. 2 *Cor.* 4 : 8-10, 16-18.
Support in death. *Ps.* 23 : 4.
A glorious resurrection. *Job* 19 : 26. *Ps.* 17 : 15. *Phil.* 3 : 21. 1 *John* 3 : 2.
A kingdom. *Heb.* 12 : 28. *Rev.* 5 : 10.
A crown. 2 *Tim.* 4 : 7, 8. *Jas.* 1 : 12.
Give diligence to attain to. 2 *Pet.* 1 : 10, 11.
Strive to maintain. *Heb.* 3 : 14, 18.
Confident hope in God restores. *Ps.* 42 : 11.
Exemplified. DAVID, *Ps.* 23 : 4. *Ps.* 73 : 24-26. PAUL, 2 *Tim.* 1 : 12. 2 *Tim.* 4 : 18.

PRIVILEGES OF SAINTS

Abiding in Christ. *John* 15 : 4, 5.
Partaking of the Divine nature. 2 *Pet.* 1 : 4.
Access to God by Christ. *Eph.* 3 : 12.
Being of the household of God. *Eph.* 2 : 19.
Membership with the Church of the first-born. *Heb.* 12 : 23.

Having

Christ for their Shepherd. *Isa.* 40 : 11, with *John* 10 : 14, 16.
Christ for their Intercessor. *Rom.* 8 : 34. *Heb.* 7 : 25. 1 *John* 2 : 1.
The promises of God. 2 *Cor.* 7 : 1. 2 *Pet.* 1 : 4.
The possession of all things. 1 *Cor.* 3 : 21, 22.
All things working together for their good. *Rom.* 8 : 28. 2 *Cor.* 4 : 15-17.
Their names written in the book of life. *Rev.* 13 : 8. *Rev.* 20 : 15.

Having God for their

King. *Ps.* 5 : 2. *Ps.* 44 : 4. *Isa.* 44 : 6.
Glory. *Ps.* 3 : 3. *Isa.* 60 : 19.
Salvation. *Ps.* 18 : 2. *Ps.* 27 : 1.
Father. *Deut.* 32 : 6. *Isa.* 64 : 8.
Redeemer. *Ps.* 19 : 14. *Isa.* 43 : 14.
Friend. 2 *Chron.* 20 : 7, with *Jas.* 2 : 23.
Helper. *Ps.* 33 : 20. *Heb.* 13 : 6.
Keeper. *Ps.* 121 : 4, 5.

CHRISTIAN CONDUCT

CONDUCT, CHRISTIAN

Believing God. *Mark* 11 : 22. *John* 14 : 1.
Fearing God. *Eccles.* 12 : 13. 1 *Pet.* 2 : 17.
Loving God. *Deut.* 6 : 5. *Matt.* 22 : 37.
Following God. *Eph.* 5 : 1. 1 *Pet.* 1 : 15, 16.
Obeying God. *Eccles.* 12 : 13. *Luke* 1 : 6.
Rejoicing in God. *Ps.* 33 : 1. *Hab.* 3 : 18.
Believing in Christ. *John* 6 : 29. *Gal.* 2 : 20.
Loving Christ. *John* 21 : 15. *Eph.* 6 : 24.
Following the example of Christ. *John* 13 : 15. 1 *Pet.* 2 : 21-24.
Obeying Christ. *John* 14 : 21. *John* 15 : 14.

Living

Â Â Â To Christ. *Rom.* 14 : 8. 2 *Cor.* 5 : 15.
Â Â Â Godly in Christ Jesus. 2 *Tim.* 3 : 12.
Â Â Â Unto righteousness. *Rom.* 6 : 18. 1 *Pet.* 2 : 24.
Â Â Â Soberly, righteously, and godly. *Titus* 2 : 12.

Walking

Â Â Â Worthy of God. 1 *Thess.* 2 : 12.
Â Â Â Worthy of the Lord. *Col.* 1 : 10.
Â Â Â In the Spirit. *Gal.* 5 : 25.
Â Â Â After the Spirit. *Rom.* 8 : 1.
Â Â Â In newness of life. *Rom.* 6 : 4.
Â Â Â Worthy of our vocation. *Eph.* 4 : 1.
Â Â Â As children of light. *Eph.* 5 : 8.
Rejoicing in Christ. *Phil.* 3 : 1. *Phil.* 4 : 4.
Loving one another. *John* 15 : 12. *Rom.* 12 : 10. 1 *Cor.* 13 : 3. *Eph.* 5 : 2. *Heb.* 13 : 1.
Striving for the faith. *Phil.* 1 : 27. *Jude* 3.
Putting away all sin. 1 *Cor.* 5 : 7. *Heb.* 12 : 1.
Abstaining from all appearance of evil. 1 *Thess.* 5 : 22.
Perfecting holiness. *Matt.* 5 : 48. 2 *Cor.* 7 : 1. 2 *Tim.* 3 : 17.
Hating defilement. *Jude* 23.
Following after that which is good. *Phil.* 4 : 8. 1 *Thess.* 5 : 15. 1 *Tim.* 6 : 11.
Overcoming the world. 1 *John* 5 : 4, 5.
Adorning the gospel. *Phil.* 1 : 27. *Titus* 2 : 10.
Showing a good example. 1 *Tim.* 4 : 12. 1 *Pet.* 2 : 12.
Abounding in the work of the Lord. 1 *Cor.* 15 : 58. 2 *Cor.* 8 : 7. 1 *Thess.* 4 : 1.
Shunning the wicked. *Ps.* 1 : 1. 2 *Thess.* 3 : 6.
Controlling the body. 1 *Cor.* 9 : 27. *Col.* 3 : 5.
Subduing the temper. *Eph.* 4 : 26. *Jas.* 1 : 19.
Submitting to injuries. *Matt.* 5: 39-41. 1 *Cor.* 6 : 7.

Forgiving injuries. *Matt.* 6 : 14. *Rom.* 12 : 20.

Living peaceably with all. *Rom.* 12 : 18. *Heb.* 12 : 14.

Visiting the afflicted. *Matt.* 25 : 36. *Jas.* 1 : 27.

Doing as we would be done by. *Matt.* 7 : 12 *Luke* 6 : 31.

Sympathising with others. *Rom.* 12 : 15. 1 *Thess.* 5 : 14.

Honouring others. *Ps.* 15 : 4. *Rom.* 12 : 10.

Fulfilling domestic duties. *Eph.* 6 : 1-8. 1 *Pet.* 3 : 1-7.

Submitting to Authorities. *Rom.* 13 : 1-7.

Being liberal to others. *Acts* 20 : 35. *Rom.* 12 : 13.

Being contented. *Phil.* 4 : 11. *Heb.* 13 : 5.

Blessedness of maintaining. *Ps.* 1 : 1-3. *Ps.* 19 : 9-11. *Ps.* 50 : 23. *Matt.* 5 : 3-12. *John* 15 : 10.

THE CHURCH

CHURCH, THE

Belongs to God. 1 *Tim.* 3 : 15.

The body of Christ. *Eph.* 1 : 23. *Col.* 1 : 24.

Christ the foundation-stone of. 1 *Cor* 3 : 11. *Eph.* 2 : 20. 1 *Pet.* 2 : 4, 6.

Christ, the head of. *Eph.* 1 : 22. *Eph.* 5 : 23.

Loved by Christ. *Song of Sol.* 7 : 10. *Eph.* 5 : 25.

Purchased by the blood of Christ. *Acts* 20 : 28. *Eph.* 5 : 25. *Heb.* 9 : 12.

Sanctified and cleansed by Christ. 1 *Cor.* 6 : 11. *Eph.* 5 : 26, 27.

Subject to Christ. *Rom.* 7 : 4. *Eph.* 5 : 24.

The object of the grace of God. *Isa.* 27 : 3. 2 *Cor.* 8 : 1.

Displays the wisdom of God. *Eph.* 3 : 10.

Shews forth the praises of God. *Isa.* 60 : 6.

God defends. *Ps.* 89 : 18. *Isa.* 4 : 5. *Isa.* 49 : 25. *Matt.* 16 : 18.

God provides ministers for. *Jer.* 3 : 15. *Eph.* 4 : 11, 12.

Glory to be ascribed to God by. *Eph.* 3 : 21.

Elect. 1 *Pet.* 5 : 13.

Glorious. *Ps.* 35 : 13. *Eph.* 5 : 27.

Clothed in righteousness. *Rev.* 19 : 8.

Believers continually added to, by the Lord. *Acts* 2 : 47. *Acts* 5 : 14. *Acts* 11 : 24.

Unity of. *Rom.* 12 : 5. 1 *Cor.* 10 : 17. 1 *Cor.* 12 : 12. *Gal.* 3 : 28.

Saints baptised into, by one Spirit. 1 *Cor.* 12 : 13.

Ministers commanded to feed. *Acts* 20.

Is edified by the word. 1 *Cor.* 14 : 4, 13. *Eph.* 4 : 15, 16.

The wicked persecute. *Acts* 8 : 1-3. 1 *Thess.* 2 : 14, 15.
Not to be despised. 1 *Cor.* 11 : 22.
Defiling of, will be punished. 1 *Cor.* 3 : 17.
Extent of, predicted. *Isa.* 2 : 2. *Ezek.* 17 : 22-24. *Dan.* 2 : 34, 35.

TITLES AND NAMES OF THE CHURCH

Assembly of the saints. *Ps.* 89 : 7.
Assembly of the upright. *Ps.* 111 : 1.
Body of Christ. *Eph.* 1 : 22, 23. *Col.* 1 : 24.
Branch of God's planting. *Isa.* 60 : 21.
Bride of Christ. *Rev.* 21 : 9.

ORDINANCES

BAPTISM

As administered by John. *Matt.* 3 : 5-12. *John* 3 : 23. *Acts* 13 : 24. *Acts* 19 : 4.
Sanctioned, by Christ's submission to it. *Matt.* 3 : 13-15. *Luke* 3 : 21.
Adopted by Christ. *John* 3 : 22. *John* 4 : 1, 2.
Appointed an ordinance of the Christian Church. *Matt.* 28 : 19, 20. *Mark* 16 : 15, 16.
To be administered in the name of the Father, the Son, and the Holy Spirit. *Matt.* 28 : 19.
Water the outward and visible sign in. *Acts* 8 : 36. *Acts* 10 : 47.
Regeneration, the inward and spiritual grace of. *John* 3 : 3, 5, 6. *Rom.* 6 : 3, 4, 11.
Remission of sins, signified by. *Acts* 2 : 38. *Acts* 22 : 16.
Unity of the Church effected by. 1 *Cor.* 12 : 13. *Gal.* 3 : 27, 28.
Confession of sin necessary to. *Matt.* 3 : 6.
Repentance necessary to. *Acts* 2 : 38.
Faith necessary to. *Acts* 8 : 37. *Acts* 18 : 8.
There is but one. *Eph.* 4 : 5.

Administered to

Individuals. *Acts* 8 : 38. *Acts* 9 : 18.
Households. *Acts* 16 : 15. 1 *Cor.* 1 : 16.
Emblematic of the influence of the Holy Spirit. *Matt.* 3 : 11. *Titus* 3 : 5.
Typified. 1 *Cor.* 10 : 2. 1 *Pet.* 3 : 20, 21.

COMMUNION OF THE LORD'S SUPPER

Prefigured. *Exod.* 12 : 21-28. 1 *Cor.* 5 : 7, 8.
Instituted. *Matt.* 26 : 26. 1 *Cor.* 11 : 23.
Object of. *Luke* 22 : 19. 1 *Cor.* 11 : 24, 26.

Is the communion of the body and blood of Christ. 1 *Cor.* 10 : 16.

Both bread and wine are necessary to be received in. *Matt.* 26 : 27. 1 *Cor.* 11 : 26.

Self-examination commanded before partaking of. 1 *Cor.* 11 : 28, 31.

Newness of heart and life necessary to the worthy partaking of. 1 *Cor.* 5 : 7, 8.

Partakers of, should be wholly separate unto God. 1 *Cor.* 10 : 21.

Was continually partaken of, by the Primitive Church. *Acts* 2 : 42. *Acts* 20 : 7.

Unworthy partakers of

Are guilty of the body and blood of Christ. 1 *Cor.* 11 : 27.

Discern not the Lord's body. 1 *Cor.* 11 : 29.

Are visited with judgments. 1 *Cor.* 11 : 30.

THE CHRISTIAN FELLOWSHIP

COMMUNION OF SAINTS

According to the prayer of Christ. *John* 17 : 20, 21.

Is with

God. 1 *John* 1 : 3.

Saints in heaven. *Heb.* 12 : 22-24.

Each other. *Gal.* 2 : 9. 1 *John* 1 : 3, 7.

God marks, with his approval. *Mal.* 3 : 16.

Christ is present in. *Matt.* 18 : 20.

In public and social worship. *Ps.* 34 : 3. *Ps.* 55 : 14. *Acts* 1 : 14. *Heb.* 10 : 25.

In the Lord's Supper. 1 *Cor.* 10 : 17.

In holy conversation. *Mal.* 3 : 16.

In prayer for each other. 2 *Cor.* 1 : 11. *Eph.* 6 : 18.

In exhortation. *Col.* 3 : 16. *Heb.* 10 : 25.

In mutual comfort and edification. 1 *Thess.* 4 : 18. 1 *Thess.* 5 : 11.

In mutual sympathy and kindness. *Rom.* 12 : 15. *Eph.* 4 : 32.

Delight of. *Ps.* 16 : 3. *Ps.* 42 : 4. *Ps.* 133 : 1-3. *Rom.* 15 : 32.

Exhortation to. *Eph.* 4 : 1-3.

Opposed to communion with the wicked. 2 *Cor.* 6 : 14-17. *Eph.* 5 : 11.

Exemplified. JONATHAN, 1 *Sam.* 23 : 16. DAVID, *Ps.* 119 : 63. DANIEL, *Dan.* 2 : 17, 18. APOSTLES, *Acts* 1 : 14. THE PRIMITIVE CHURCH, *Acts* 2 : 42. *Acts* 5 : 12. PAUL, *Acts* 20 : 36-38.

THE GOSPEL

Described. *Luke* 2 : 10, 11.
Foretold. *Isa.* 41 : 27. *Isa.* 52 : 7, with *Rom.* 10 : 15. *Isa.* 61 : 1-3.
Preached under the Old Testament. *Heb.* 4 : 2.
Exhibits the grace of God. *Acts* 11 : 3. *Acts* 20 : 32.
The knowledge of the glory of God is by. 2 *Cor.* 4 : 4, 6.
Life and immortality are brought to light by. 2 *Tim.* 1 : 10.
Is the power of God unto salvation. *Rom.* 1 : 16. 1 *Cor.* 1 : 18. 1 *Thess.* 1 : 5.
Is truth. *Col.* 1 : 5.
Is glorious. 2 *Cor.* 4 : 4.
Is everlasting. 1 *Pet.* 1 : 25. *Rev.* 14 : 6.
Preached by Christ. *Matt.* 4 : 23. *Mark* 1 : 14.
Ministers have dispensation to preach. 1 *Cor.* 9 : 17.
Preached beforehand to Abraham. *Gen.* 22 : 18, with *Gal.* 3 : 8.

Preached to

The Jews first. *Luke* 24 : 47. *Acts* 13 : 46. *Acts* 14 : 1. *Acts* 16 : 3. *Acts* 17 : 1, and 2. *Acts* 18 : 4. *Acts* 19 : 8. *Acts* 28 : 17.
The Gentiles. *Mark* 13 : 10. *Gal.* 2 : 2.
The poor. *Matt.* 11 : 5. *Luke* 4 : 18.
Every creature. *Mark* 16 : 15. *Col.* 1 : 23.
Must be believed. *Mark* 1 : 15. *Heb.* 4 : 2.
Brings peace. *Luke* 2 : 10, 14. *Eph.* 6 : 15.
Produces hope. *Col.* 1 : 23.
Saints have fellowship in. *Phil.* 1 : 5.
There is fulness of blessing in. *Rom.* 15 : 29.

Those who receive, should

Adhere to the truth of. *Gal.* 1 : 6, 7. *Gal.* 2 : 14.
Not be ashamed of. *Rom.* 1 : 16.
Live in subjection to. 2 *Cor.* 9 : 13.
Have their conversation becoming. *Phil.* 1 : 27.
Earnestly contend for the faith of. *Phil.* 1 : 17, 27. *Jude* 3.
Sacrifice friends and property for. *Mark* 10 : 29.
Sacrifice life itself for. *Mark* 8 : 35.
Profession of, attended by afflictions. 2 *Tim.* 1 : 8.
Promises to sufferers for. *Mark* 8 : 35. *Mark* 10 : 30.
Be careful not to hinder. 1 *Cor.* 9 : 12.
Is hid to them that are lost. 2 *Cor.* 4 : 3.
Testifies to the final judgment. *Rom.* 2 : 16.
Let him who preaches another, be accursed. *Gal.* 1 : 8.
Awful consequences of not obeying. 2 *Thess.* 1 : 8, 9.

Is called, the
Dispensation of the grace of God. *Eph.* 3 : 2.
Gospel of peace. *Eph.* 6 : 15.
Gospel of God. *Rom.* 1 : 1. 1 *Thess.* 2 : 8. 1 *Pet.* 4 : 17.
Gospel of Jesus Christ. *Rom.* 1 : 9, 16. 2 *Cor.* 2 : 12. 1 *Thess.* 3 : 2.
Gospel of the grace of God. *Acts* 20 : 24.
Gospel of the kingdom. *Matt.* 24 : 14.
Gospel of salvation. *Eph.* 1 : 13.
Glorious gospel of Christ. 2 *Cor.* 4 : 4.
Preaching of Jesus Christ. *Rom.* 16 : 25.
Mystery of Christ. *Eph.* 3 : 4.
Mystery of the gospel. *Eph.* 6 : 19.
Word of God. 1 *Thess.* 2 : 13.
Word of Christ. *Col.* 3 : 16.
Word of grace. *Acts* 14 : 3. *Acts* 20 : 32.
Word of salvation. *Acts* 13 : 26.
Word of reconciliation. 2 *Cor.* 5 : 19.
Word of truth. *Eph.* 1 : 13. 2 *Cor.* 6 : 7.
Word of faith. *Rom.* 10 : 8.
Word of life. *Phil.* 2 : 16.
Ministration of the Spirit. 2 *Cor.* 3 : 8.
Doctrine according to godliness. 1 *Tim.* 6 : 3.
Form of sound words. 2 *Tim.* 1 : 13.
Rejection of, by many, foretold. *Isa.* 53 : 1, with *Rom.* 10 : 15, 16.
Rejection of, by the Jews, a means of blessing to the Gentiles. *Rom.* 11 : 28.

MINISTERS

Commanded. *Matt.* 28 : 19. *Mark* 16 : 15.
Warranted by predictions concerning the Heathen, etc. *Isa.* 42 : 10-12. *Isa.* 66 : 19.
Is according to the purpose of God. *Luke* 24 : 46, 47. *Gal.* 1 : 15, 16. *Col.* 1 : 25-27.
Directed by the Holy Ghost. *Acts* 13 : 2.
Required. *Luke* 10 : 2. *Rom.* 10 : 14, 15.
The Holy Ghost calls to. *Acts* 13 : 2.

THE SECOND COMING

SECOND COMING OF CHRIST, THE

Time of, unknown. *Matt.* 24 : 36. *Mark* 13 : 32.

Called the
Times of refreshing from the presence of the Lord. *Acts* 3 : 19.
Times of the restitution of all things. *Act* 3 : 21, with *Rom.* 8 : 21.
Last time. 1 *Pet.* 1 : 5.
Appearing of Jesus Christ. 1 *Pet.* 1 : 7.
Revelation of Jesus Christ. 1 *Pet.* 1 : 13. 1 *Cor.* 1 : 7.
Glorious appearing of the great God and our Saviour. *Titus* 2 : 13.
Coming of the day of God. 2 *Pet.* 3 : 12.
Day of our Lord Jesus Christ. 1 *Cor.* 1 : 8.

Foretold by
> Prophets. *Dan.* 7 : 13. *Jude* 14.
> Himself. *Matt.* 25 : 31. *John* 14 : 3.
> Apostles. *Acts* 3 : 20. 1 *Tim.* 6 : 14.
> Angels. *Acts* 1 : 10, 11.

Signs preceding. *Matt.* 24 : 3, etc.

The manner of ;
> In clouds. *Matt.* 24 : 30. *Matt.* 26 : 24.
> *Rev.* 1 : 7.
> In the glory of his Father. *Matt.* 16 : 17
> In his own glory. *Matt.* 25 : 31.
> In flaming fire. 2 *Thess.* 1 : 8.
> With power and great glory. *Matt.* 24 :
> 30.
> As He ascended. *Acts* 1 : 9, 11.
> With a shout and the voice of the Arch-
> angel, etc. 1 *Thess.* 4 : 16.
> Accompanied by Angels. *Matt.* 16 : 27.
> *Matt.* 25 : 31. *Mark* 8 : 38. 2 *Thess.*
> 1 : 7.
> With his saints. 1 *Thess.* 3 : 13. *Jude*
> 14.
> Suddenly. *Mark* 13 : 36.
> Unexpectedly. *Matt.* 24 : 44. *Luke* 12 :
> 40.
> As a thief in the night. 1 *Thess.* 5 : 2.
> 2 *Pet.* 3 : 10. *Rev.* 16 : 15.
> As the lightning. *Matt.* 24 : 27.

The heavens and earth shall be dissolved,
etc. 2 *Pet.* 3 : 10, 12.
They who shall have died in Christ shall
rise first at. 1 *Thess.* 4 : 16.
The saints alive at, shall be caught up to
meet him. 1 *Thess.* 4 : 17.
Is not to make atonement. *Heb.* 9 : 28,
with *Rom.* 6 : 9, 10, and *Heb.* 10 : 14.

The purposes of, are to
> Complete the salvation of saints. *Heb.*
> 9 : 28, 1 *Pet.* 1 : 5.
> Be glorified in his saints. 2 *Thess.* 1 : 10.
> Be admired in them that believe. 2
> *Thess.* 1 : 10.
> Bring to light the hidden things of dark-
> ness, etc. 1 *Cor.* 4 : 5.
> Judge. *Ps.* 50 : 3, 4, with *John* 5 : 22.
> 2 *Tim.* 4 : 1. *Jude* 15. *Rev.* 20 : 11-13.
> Reign. *Isa.* 24 : 23. *Dan.* 7 : 14. *Rev.*
> 11 : 15.
> Destroy death. 1 *Cor.* 15 : 23, 26.

Every eye shall see him at. *Rev.* 1 : 7.
Should be always considered as at hand.
Rom. 13 : 12. *Phil.* 4 : 5. *Pet.* 4 : 7.
Blessedness of being prepared for. *Matt.*
24 : 46. *Luke* 12 : 37, 38.

Saints
> Assured of. *Job* 19 : 25, 26.
> Love. 2 *Tim.* 4 : 8.
> Look for. *Phil.* 3 : 20. *Titus* 2 : 13.
> Wait for. 1 *Cor.* 1 : 7. 1 *Thess.* 1 : 10.
> Haste unto. 2 *Pet.* 3 : 12.
> Pray for. *Rev.* 22 : 20.
> Should be ready for. *Matt.* 24 : 44. *Luke*
> 12 : 40.

Should watch for. *Matt.* 24 : 42. *Mark*
13 : 35-37. *Luke* 21 : 36.

Should be patient unto. 2 *Thess.* 3 : 5.
Jas. 5 : 7, 8.

Shall be preserved unto. *Phil.* 1 : 6. 2
Tim. 4 : 18. 1 *Pet.* 1 : 5. *Jude* 24.

Shall not be ashamed at. 1 *John* 2 : 28.

Shall be blameless at. 1 *Cor.* 1 : 8. 1
Thess. 3 : 13. 1 *Thess.* 5 : 23. *Jude* 24.

Shall be like him at. *Phil.* 3 : 21. 1
John 3 : 2.

Shall see him as He is, at. 1 *John* 3 : 2.

Shall appear with him in glory at. *Col.*
3 : 4.

Shall receive a crown of glory at. 2 *Tim.*
4 : 8. 1 *Pet.* 5 : 4.

Shall reign with him at. *Dan.* 7 : 27.
2 *Tim.* 2 : 12. *Rev.* 5 : 10. *Rev.* 20 : 6.
Rev. 22 : 5.

Faith of, shall be found unto praise at.
1 *Pet.* 1 : 7.

The wicked

Scoff at. 2 *Pet.* 3 : 3, 4.

Presume upon the delay of. *Matt.* 24 :
48.

Shall be surprised by. *Matt.* 24 : 37-39.
1 *Thess.* 5 : 3. 2 *Pet.* 3 : 10.

Shall be punished at. 2 *Thess.* 1 : 8, 9.

The man of sin to be destroyed at. 2 *Thess.*
2 : 8.

THE RESURRECTION OF THE BODY

RESURRECTION, THE

A doctrine of the Old Testament. *Job*
19 : 26. *Ps.* 49 : 15. *Isa.* 26 : 19. *Dan.*
12 : 2. *Gen.* 22 : 5. *Heb.* 11 : 19.

A first principle of the gospel. *Heb.* 6 : 1, 2.

Expected by the Jews. *John* 11 : 24. *Heb.*
11 : 35.

Denied by the Sadducees. *Matt.* 22 : 23.
Luke 20 : 27. *Acts* 23 : 8.

Explained away by false teachers. 2 *Tim.*
2 : 18.

Called in question by some in the primitive
Church. 1 *Cor.* 15 : 12.

Is not incredible. *Mark* 12 : 24. *Acts* 26 : 8.

Is not contrary to reason. *John* 12 : 24.
1 *Cor.* 15 : 35-44.

Assumed and proved by our Lord. *Matt.*
22 : 29-32. *Luke* 14 : 14. *John* 5 : 28, 29.

Preached by the Apostles. *Acts* 4 : 2.
Acts 17 : 18. *Acts* 24 : 15.

Credibility of, shown by resurrection of
individuals. *Matt.* 9 : 25. *Matt.* 27 : 53.
Luke 7 : 14. *John* 11 : 44. *Heb.* 11 : 35.

Certainty of, proved by the resurrection of
Christ. 1 *Cor.* 15 : 12-20.

Effected by the power of

God. *Matt.* 22 : 29.

Christ. *John* 5 : 28, 29. *John* 6 : 39, 40,
44.

The Holy Ghost. *Rom.* 8 : 11.
Shall be of all the dead. *John* 5 : 28. *Acts*
24 : 15. *Rev.* 20 : 13.

Saints in, shall

Rise through Christ. *John* 11 : 25.
Acts 4 : 2. 1 *Cor.* 15 : 21, 22.
Rise first. 1 *Cor.* 15 : 23. 1 *Thess.* 4 : 16.
Rise to eternal life. *Dan.* 12 : 2. *John*
5 : 29.
Be glorified with Christ. *Col.* 3 : 4.
Be as the angels. *Matt.* 22 : 30.
Have incorruptible bodies. 1 *Cor.* 15 :
42.
Have glorious bodies. 1 *Cor.* 15 : 43.
Have powerful bodies. 1 *Cor.* 15 : 43.
Have spiritual bodies. 1 *Cor.* 15 : 44.
Have bodies like Christ's. *Phil.* 3 : 21.
Be recompensed. *Luke* 14 : 14.
Saints should look forward to. *Dan.* 12 :
13. *Phil.* 3 : 11.
Of saints shall be followed by the change
of those then alive. 1 *Cor.* 15 : 51, with
1 *Thess.* 4 : 17.

The preaching of, caused

Mocking. *Acts* 17 : 32.
Persecution. *Acts* 23 : 6. *Acts* 24 : 11-15.
Blessedness of those who have part in the
first. *Rev.* 20 : 6.

Of the wicked, shall be to

Shame and everlasting contempt. *Dan.*
12 : 2.
Damnation. *John* 5 : 29.
Illustrative of the new-birth. *John* 5 : 25.
Illustrated. *Ezek.* 37 : 1-10. 1 *Cor.* 15 :
36, 37.
Associated with the Feast of Tabernacles.
Lev. 23. *Isa.* 25 : 6-9. 1 *Cor.* 15 : 54.

THE SAVED

REWARD OF SAINTS, THE

Is from God. *Col.* 3 : 24. *Heb.* 11 : 6.
Is of grace, through faith alone. *Rom.* 4 :
4, 5, 16. *Rom.* 11 : 6.
Is of God's good pleasure. *Luke* 12 : 32.
Prepared by God. *Heb.* 11 : 16.
Prepared by Christ. *John* 14 : 2.
As servants of Christ. *Col.* 3 : 24.
Not on account of their merits. *Rom.* 4 :
4, 5.

Described as

Being with Christ. *John* 12 : 26. *John*
14 : 3. *Phil.* 1 : 23. 1 *Thess.* 4 : 17.
Beholding the face of God. *Ps.* 17 : 15.
Matt. 5 : 8. *Rev.* 22 : 4.
Beholding the glory of Christ. *John* 17 :
24.
Being glorified with Christ. *Rom.* 8 : 17,
18. *Col.* 3 : 4.
Sitting in judgment with Christ. *Luke*
22 : 30, with 1 *Cor.* 6 : 2.

Reigning with Christ. 2 *Tim.* 2 : 12. *Rev.* 5 : 10. *Rev.* 20 : 4.
Reigning for ever and ever. *Rev.* 22 : 5.
A crown of righteousness. 2 *Tim.* 4 : 8.
A crown of glory. 1 *Pet.* 5 : 4.
A crown of life. *Jas.* 1 : 12. *Rev.* 2 : 10.
An incorruptible crown. 1 *Cor.* 9 : 25.
Joint heirship with Christ. *Rom.* 8 : 17.
Inheritance of all things. *Rev.* 21 : 7.
Inheritance with saints in light. *Acts* 20 : 32. *Acts* 26 : 18. *Col.* 1 : 12.
Inheritance eternal. *Heb.* 9 : 15.
Inheritance incorruptible, etc. 1 *Pet.* 1 : 4.
A kingdom. *Matt.* 25 : 34. *Luke* 22 : 29.
A kingdom immovable. *Heb.* 12 : 28.
Shining as the stars. *Dan.* 12 : 3.
Everlasting light. *Isa.* 60 : 19.
Everlasting life. *Luke* 18 : 30. *Rom.* 6 : 23.
An enduring substance. *Heb.* 10 : 34.
A house, eternal in the heavens. 2 *Cor.* 5 : 1.
A city which hath foundations. *Heb.* 11 : 10.
Entering into the joy of the Lord. *Matt.* 25 : 21, with *Heb.* 12 : 2.
Rest. *Heb.* 4 : 9. *Rev.* 14 : 13.
Fulness of joy. *Ps.* 16 : 11.
The prize of the high calling of God in Christ. *Phil.* 3 : 14.
Treasure in heaven. *Matt.* 19 : 21. *Luke* 12 : 33.
An eternal weight of glory. 2 *Cor.* 4 : 17.
Is great. *Matt.* 5 : 12. *Luke* 6 : 35. *Heb.* 10 : 35.
Is full. 2 *John* 8.
Is sure. *Prov.* 11 : 18.
Is satisfying. *Ps.* 17 : 15.
Is inestimable. *Isa.* 64 : 4, with 1 *Cor.* 2 : 9.
Saints may feel confident of. *Ps.* 73 : 24. 2 *Cor.* 5 : 1. 2 *Tim.* 4 : 8.
Hope of, a cause of rejoicing. *Rom.* 5 : 2.
Be careful not to lose. 2 *John* 8.

The prospect of, should lead to

Diligence. 2 *John* 8.
Pressing forward. *Phil.* 3 : 14.
Enduring suffering for Christ. 2 *Cor.* 4 : 16-18. *Heb.* 11 : 26.
Faithfulness unto death. *Rev.* 2 : 10.
Present afflictions not to be compared with. *Rom.* 8 : 18.
Shall be given at the second coming of Christ. *Matt.* 16 : 27. *Rev.* 22 : 12. 2 *Tim.* 4 : 1, 8.

HEAVEN

Created by God. *Gen.* 1 : 1. *Rev.* 10 : 6.
Everlasting. *Ps.* 89 : 29. 2 *Cor.* 5 : 1.
Immeasurable. *Jer.* 31 : 37.
High. *Ps.* 103 : 11. *Isa.* 57 : 15.
Holy. *Deut.* 26 : 15. *Ps.* 20 : 6. *Isa.* 57 : 15.
God's dwelling-place. 1 *Kings* 8 : 30. *Matt.* 6 : 9.
God's throne. *Isa.* 66 : 1, with *Acts* 7 : 49

God

Is the Lord of. *Dan.* 5 : 23. *Matt.* 11 : 25.
Reigns in. *Ps.* 11 : 4. *Ps.* 135 : 6. *Dan.*
4 : 35.
Fills. 1 *Kings* 8 : 27. *Jer.* 23 : 24.
Answers his people from. 1 *Chron.* 21 :
26. 2 *Chron.* 7 : 14. *Neh.* 9 : 27. *Ps.*
20 : 6.
Sends his judgments from. *Gen.* 19 : 24.
1 *Sam.* 2 : 10. *Dan.* 4 : 13, 14. *Rom.* 1 :
18.

Christ

As Mediator, entered into. *Acts* 3 : 21.
Heb. 6 : 20. *Heb.* 9 : 12, 24.
Is all-powerful in. *Matt.* 28 : 18. 1 *Pet.*
3 : 22.
Angels are in. *Matt.* 18 : 10. *Mark* 24 : 36.
Names of saints are written in. *Luke* 10 :
20. *Heb.* 12 : 23.
Saints rewarded in. *Matt.* 5 : 12. 1 *Pet.*
1 : 4.
Repentance occasions joy in. *Luke* 15 : 7.
Lay up treasure in. *Matt.* 6 : 20. *Luke*
12 : 33.
Flesh and blood cannot inherit. 1 *Cor.*
15 : 50.
Happiness of, described. *Rev.* 7 : 16, 17.

Is called

A garner. *Matt.* 3 : 12.
The kingdom of Christ and of God. *Eph.*
5 : 5.
The Father's house. *John* 14 : 2.
A heavenly country. *Heb.* 11 : 16.
A rest. *Heb.* 4 : 9.
Paradise. 2 *Cor.* 12 : 2, 4.
The wicked excluded from. *Gal.* 5 : 21.
Eph. 5 : 5. *Rev.* 22 : 15.
Enoch and Elijah were translated into.
Gen. 5 : 24, with *Heb.* 11 : 5. 2 *Kings*
2 : 11.

THE LOST

PUNISHMENT OF THE WICKED, THE

Is from God. *Lev.* 26 : 18. *Isa.* 13 : 11.

On account of their

Sin. *Lam.* 3 : 39.
Iniquity. *Jer.* 36 : 31. *Amos* 3 : 2.
Idolatry. *Lev.* 26 : 30. *Isa.* 10 : 10, 11.
Rejection of the law of God. *Hos.* 4 :
6-9.
Ignorance of God. 2 *Thess.* 1 : 8.
Evil ways and doings. *Jer.* 21 : 14.
Hos. 4 : 9. *Hos.* 12 : 2.
Pride. *Isa.* 10 : 12. *Isa.* 24 : 21.
Unbelief. *Rom.* 11 : 20. *Heb.* 3 : 18, 19

Covetousness. *Isa.* 57 : 17. *Jer.* 51 : 13.
Oppressing. *Isa.* 49 : 26. *Jer.* 30 : 16, 20.
Persecuting. *Jer.* 11 : 21, 22. *Matt.* 23 : 34-36.
Disobeying God. *Neh.* 9 : 26, 27. *Eph.* 5 : 6.
Disobeying the gospel. 2 *Thess.* 1 : 8.
Is the fruit of their sin. *Job* 4 : 8. *Prov.* 22 : 8. *Rom.* 6 : 21. *Gal.* 6 : 8.
Is the reward of their sin. *Ps.* 91 : 8. *Isa.* 3 : 11. *Jer.* 16 : 18. *Rom.* 6 : 23. *Heb.* 2 : 2.
Often brought about by their evil designs. *Esther* 7 : 10. *Ps.* 37 : 15. *Ps.* 57 : 6.
Often commences in this life. *Prov.* 11 : 31.

In this life by

Sickness. *Lev.* 26 : 16. *Ps.* 78 : 50.
Famine. *Lev.* 26 : 19, 20, 26, 29. *Ps.* 107 : 34.
Noisome beasts. *Lev.* 26 : 22.
War. *Lev.* 26 : 25, 32, 33. *Jer.* 6 : 4.
Deliverance unto enemies. *Neh.* 9 : 27.
Fear. *Lev.* 26 : 36, 37. *Job* 18 : 11.
Trouble and distress. *Isa.* 8 : 22. *Zeph.* 1 : 15.
Cutting off. *Ps.* 94 : 23.
Bringing down their pride. *Isa.* 13 : 11.
Future, shall be awarded by Christ. *Matt.* 16 : 27. *Matt.* 25 : 31, 41.

Future, described as

Hell. *Matt.* 5 : 29. *Luke* 12 : 5.
Darkness. *Matt.* 8 : 12. 2 *Pet.* 2 : 17.
Resurrection of damnation. *John* 5 : 29.
Rising to shame and everlasting contempt. *Dan.* 12 : 2.
Everlasting destruction. *Ps.* 52 : 5. *Ps.* 92 : 7. 2 *Thess.* 1 : 9.
Everlasting fire. *Matt.* 25 : 41. *Jude* 7.
Eternal death. *Rom.* 6 : 23. *Rev.* 21 : 8.
Damnation of hell. *Matt.* 23 : 33.
Eternal damnation. *Matt.* 3 : 29.
Blackness of darkness. 2 *Pet.* 2 : 17. *Jude* 13.
Everlasting burnings. *Isa.* 33 : 14.
Wine of the wrath of God. *Rev.* 14 : 10.
Torment with fire. *Rev.* 14 : 10.
Torment for ever and ever. *Rev.* 14 : 11.
The righteousness of God requires. 2 *Thess.* 1 : 6.
Often sudden and unexpected. *Ps.* 35 : 8. *Ps.* 64 : 7. *Prov.* 29 : 1. 1 *Thess.* 5 : 3.

Shall be

According to their deeds. *Matt.* 16 : 27. *Rom.* 2 : 6, 9. 2 *Cor.* 5 : 10.
According to the knowledge possessed by them. *Luke* 12 : 47, 48.
Increased by neglect of privileges. *Matt.* 11 : 21-24. *Luke* 10 : 13-15.

31

Without mitigation. *Luke* 16 : 23-26
Accompanied by remorse. *Isa.* 66 : 24
with *Mark* 9 : 44.
No combination avails against. *Prov.* 11 :
21.
Deferred, emboldens them in sin. *Eccles.*
8 : 11.
Should be a warning to others. *Num.*
26 : 10. *Jude* 7.
Consummated at the day of judgment.
Matt. 25 : 31, 46. *Rom.* 2 : 5, 16. 2 *Pet.*
2 : 9.

THE JUDGMENT

JUDGMENT, THE

Predicted in the Old Testament. 1 *Chron.*
16 : 33. *Ps.* 9 : 7. *Ps.* 96 : 13. *Eccles.* 3 :
17.
A first principle of the gospel. *Heb.* 6 : 2.
A day appointed for. *Acts* 17 : 31. *Rom.*
2 : 16.
Time of, unknown to us. *Mark* 13 : 32.

Called, the

Day of wrath. *Rom.* 2 : 5. *Rev.* 6 : 17.
Revelation of the righteous judgment of
God. *Rom.* 2 : 5.
Day of judgment and perdition of un-
godly men. 2 *Pet.* 3 : 7.
Day of destruction. *Job* 21 : 30.
Judgment of the great day. *Jude* 6.
Shall be administered by Christ. *John* 5 :
22, 27. *Acts* 10 : 42. *Rom.* 14 : 10. 2 *Cor.*
5 : 10.
Saints shall sit with Christ in. 1 *Cor.* 6 : 2.
Rev. 20 : 4.
Shall take place at the coming of Christ.
Matt. 25 : 31. 2 *Tim.* 4 : 1.
Of Heathens, by the law of conscience.
Rom. 2 : 12, 14, 15.
Of Jews, by the law of Moses. *Rom.* 2 : 12.
Of Christians, by the gospel. *Jas.* 2 : 12.

Shall be held upon

All nations. *Matt.* 25 : 32.
All men. *Heb.* 9 : 27. *Heb.* 12 : 23.
Small and great. *Rev.* 20 : 12.
The righteous and wicked. *Eccles.* 3 : 17.
Quick and dead. 2 *Tim.* 4 : 1. 1 *Pet.*
4 : 5.
Shall be in righteousness. *Ps.* 98 : 9. *Acts*
17 : 31.
The books shall be opened at. *Dan.* 7 : 10.